AF265603

SNOW MOON SWIMMER

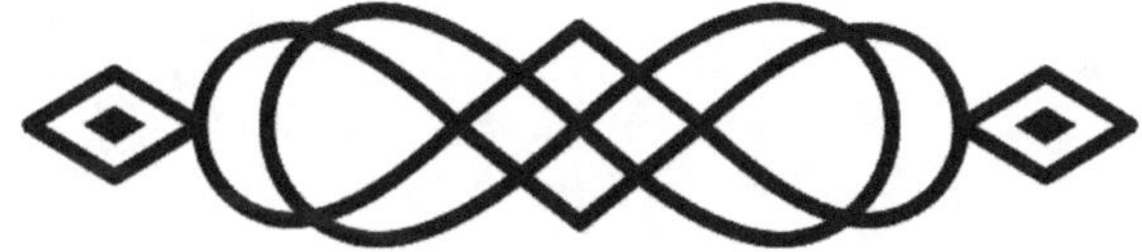

Bethanie Mitchell

ALSO BY BETHANIE MITCHELL
Antara

Copyright Bethanie Mitchell
All rights reserved. No part of this work may be reproduced or transmitted in any form or by any means, electronic or mechanical, including photocopy, recording, or any information storage or retrieval system without permission in writing from the publisher or author.

Bethanie Mitchell has asserted her right to be identified as the author of this work in accordance with the Federal Copyright Act 1976.

Photography: Bethanie Mitchell

ISBN: 9780578290096

Author: Bethanie Mitchell
Address: Shoreline, WA, USA
First Published: April 2022

Table of Contents:

For Yarrow

A Steel Home

Machine guns fire through TV static.
Olive shag rug, all family secrets hide there.
Howling winds through the corn fields
pigs squeal down the road.
Castration is seasonal,
Ah, it's fall.
The smell of flavorless meat permeates cut grass in the
summer.
My father's Marlboro-infused sweat.
Salt of the earth, I am from.
Miles away, nobody near.
A weeping willow branch for a swing,
My only real friend.
Sister is out in the forest.
I will meet her there, after I finish *Where the Red Fern
Grows*.
Mother peers out the kitchen window at a fall sunset,
Dreaming while drying the dishes.
The smell of chlorine is permanent on me.
Corn or chlorine.
Click or outsider.
Pantera or church.
The brick layer is KING.
Money house perfection, the perfect lie hides in the olive
shag rug.
Teach or tractor.
Military or jail.
Crack or baseball.
There are few opportunities here.
 Big hearts, small minds.
 I have lived around the world.
 Still, I am never settled.
 The perfect imperfect place.
 A black hole.
 I miss nothing.

I miss everything.
I wish I never lived there.
I wish I never left the pumpkin patch.
Conflicting, the prison I'm from.
Doing time on a probate.
I'll continue to wander until I find another
Pumpkin Capitol of the World.

Freedom

Barbara...an oasis in my prison on Bank Street.
Fortitude given like a rock-hard avocado.
Freedom as fetus, ready to burst.
Abort ties, pick up checks.
Stack jeans, rolling wheels.
All in the name of FREEDOM.
Will I ever fully arrive?
Cages like peanut butter stuck on the roof of your mouth.
This is the feeling of loss of freedom.
Old woman, pot belly,
Bag from Beirut
Representation like a Greek Key.
It's a maze
that hexagonal corn row to FREEDOM.
Open doors can come through risk and dictatorship.
Where there is so much law there is no law.
Hezbollah gives me hutzpah
Better go meet em'
Barbara naked in the forest Upstate New York
Young Asian lover
Mother of none.
Giver of tea and talk
only at 5pm on Thursdays
The impetus.
A little light peeking through the curtain was
Like I made it to the border.
Hezbollah, rush beyond US border
Snap snap,
Click click.
Beirut Barbara
It was the day I heard of the foreign word FREEDOM
And it will be gifted to me.
Trying to arrive is like removing peanut butter on the roof of
my mouth.
It's tedious business

...to find FREEDOM.
Snow crystal shards
drop like knives from the sky on my path to FREEEDOM.
Democracy juggles Punji sticks before I pass Gate 88 at JFK.
Hezbollah waves a white flag
Snap snap.
Click click.
Wind that roll
use those internal walls built by stilettos strong as hammers
I have arrived
Land in dictatorship
Golden ticket.
US Passport—
We are all entitled
But few find freedom
Beirut Bag, Barbara
Here it is, Bethanie.
Go and grab it
Return your MOMA tickets
Enjoy your FREEDOM
The self-built museum only open to you.

Moon Swimmer

Spiral curls
She is wild
Skittish, full, and seafaring with foam
at the side of her left lip.
She is wild and she will be mine,
or so I dream.
Why would I pluck a thorn from its stalk,
Take her freedom?
Just so I can talk and say she is mine?
She is wild.
She is unapproachable nucleus.
She is lonely nuclear hot lava love.
She wonders why she salvages backed into a corner.
Drippings down a drainpipe to keep the underworld
hydrated.
Wild woman with no glass palace,
No entrance
She would steal the show during showtime
and the herd would cower.
It's all her
It's all her power.
If you were owned
Your life would become a burned up throne
Its ashes wouldn't fertilize Demeter's crops
or drench Hades loveless hyssops.

Swamp Woman

Twinkling rippled cellophane
Covers moon brie
Sloppy swamp woman
Seaweed dangles and reflects from her tentacles.
Black silhouette warped in the blue.
After sunrise
hardboiled Corona tan
melts away with White Rabbit blaring in the background
Feeding rays - razor straight from your eyes.
Hexagonal kaleidoscope vision
Opens up the 70's sunset
We can all see the sea now.

The Mad Man of Rangoon

Betel nut juice or blood, perhaps a cocktail of both.
Shrills and thumping bodies like rusty Russian rockets on
takeoff make like falling stars.
Cross stitched heart equals fragile.
Blinded by the light of a sword no it was the belues* dark
knight holding
with karmic freedom
Was it your father?
Crocheted betle nut juice or warning blood?
Perhaps a cocktail designed of both decors.
the hall corner in the dark.
Heavy breath urgency but slow to the next step like its paved
with glass shards and bells that sing of arrival.
Hot clammy dark
The air fills of petrol fumes mixed with peanut oil. Smells
remind me I'm still in Rangoon and this staircase is longer
than the Mandalay highway and possibly more dangerous.
A faint light escapes the cracked door
Will we cross the border safely?
It's only 88th Street.

His doughboy frame seems to expand.
The voice says, "Fuck your mother."
My hand slides on the door handle
We fall once again into a Chinese black box.
Oh, the small living room.

Another night.
Shrills like sounds of rusty Russian tanks and thumping like
cosmic debris on Soviet rockets
is the backdrop
Apartment 54 at dinner time
With a cross stitched heart fragile and unraveling.
We peek out and are blinded by the swords glare.

Insane dark knight from Insein Prison*.
Tatmadaw * holds karmic freedom
We escape the mouth of a shark
Thank you, little China man.
The new renter who appears deaf to Burmese for Mandarin
cackles from his phone call
Is it luck?
But the eye is universal and he will be blinded by the sword
as well.
Tatmawdaw* gifts for the expat or will it disappear
for the Chinese special relationship is clear.

The North Sea Swimmer

Painfully peppered by lions mane tips.
After one shocking plunge into your pelagic morphine soup.
Ice queen.
I am the ice queen!
The coronation entails
minutes of pain and hours of flagellation.
Au fait sea swimmer.
I am, but you are notorious.
Truth Na Maoile*
You have killed the Children of Lir*
and swallowed Princess Victoria.
This sea swimmer, insignificant
and respectful rides
Your cold hands rocking.
Crash!
You aggressively push me along.
Sick and drunk on an elixir of your salty broth.
Numb and euphoric while living a lifetime in one crossing.
The toughest of teachers that is the most beautiful.
Dark sugar land awaits and breakfast in Belfast.

Richmond Beach Wave

A crest for spirit life.
Cold salty Poseidon roars.
Roughs sleep then linger.
Foaming lips part, rippling hiss.
Walls of water meet sailors.

My Time

A quivering wave
Crisp and cold with perfect form
at the swimmer's beach.

88

On the Chindwin* I
saw a sleepy palm sway
and drop its great fruit.

The Salish Sea, April 1922

A sea I knew well
makes all the ladies cry because
it's cold and boundless.

My Burma Man

What I offer you but a hug
A mind's fast dark flight
A tired-skinned trail of drug
Skinny on a train fight.

No word salad supper
Overt nuts out of shell
I'm no foreigner
And this isn't hell.

Sagaing Hill calls you hard
Saffron robes blow high
Olive rags stiff as military guard
More jeweled than Thai

A little compass
Left of quietness

Snow Moon Swimmer

Snow moon swim
on a Wednesday night.
                    Wednesdays
in the Salish Sea.

Swim trials for a dark sea in late summer.
The North Channel will be the most cavillous of judges.

Talk of a North Channel Sea Swimmer
Depicts all that is wrong with
                    Hump Day
                    Humor

It's the Salish Orcas who rule
                    Wednesdays
S i n g i n g to swimmers.

The Lion's Mane oversee Irish nights
Acting out witchcraft in their murky wild sea.

North Channel Sea Captain as
                    Soothsayer.

We haven't met yet.

I'm c h u r n i n g my strokes during seasonal moons
in the Salish Sea.

Preparing for our future engagement that begins on
Copeland Island.

Definitions:

* Insein Prison - a prison in Yangon, Myanmar
* belues - Burmese mythical devil
* Tatmawdaw - Burmese military
* Truth Na Maoile - Gaelic for North Channel
* Children of Lir- Irish myth
* Chindwin - A river in northern Myanmar
* Sagaing Hill - A hill in northern Myanmar

www.ingramcontent.com/pod-product-compliance
Lightning Source LLC
Chambersburg PA
CBHW051015050726
47592CB00007B/2855